MATH YOU WILL ACTUALLY USE™

USING MATH IN COOKING

LINDA R. BAKER

rosen publishing's
rosen central®
New York

Published in 2018 by The Rosen Publishing Group, Inc.
29 East 21st Street, New York, NY 10010

First Edition

Library of Congress Cataloging-in-Publication Data

Names: Baker, Linda R.
Title: Using math in cooking / Linda R. Baker.
Description: New York : Rosen Publishing, 2018 | Series: Math you will actually use | Includes bibliographical references and index.
Identifiers: ISBN 9781499438581 (library bound) | ISBN 9781499438567 (pbk.) | ISBN 9781499438574 (6 pack)
Subjects: LCSH: Cooking—Mathematics—Juvenile literature.
Classification: LCC TX652.5 B35 2018 | DDC 641.501'51—dc23

Manufactured in the United States of America

METRIC CONVERSION CHART	
1 inch = 2.54 centimeters; 25.4 millimeters	1 cup = 250 milliliters
1 foot = 30.48 centimeters	1 ounce = 28 grams
1 yard = .914 meters	1 fluid ounce = 30 milliliters
1 square foot = .093 square meters	1 teaspoon = 5 milliliters
1 square mile = 2.59 square kilometers	1 tablespoon = 15 milliliters
1 ton = .907 metric tons	1 quart = .946 liters
1 pound = 454 grams	355 degrees Fahrenheit = 180 degrees Celsius
1 mile = 1.609 kilometers	

CONTENTS

Introduction

Eliza does not understand why she has to study math. It's confusing, and she cannot see how it could be useful in her life. In the morning, she thinks she understands what the teacher is showing her because her teacher relates the math problems to real-life situations. But when she gets home, she can't seem to remember how to work the problems. She is frustrated, and when she asks her parents for help, it gets even worse. When they learned math, it was taught differently, so they do not understand her homework any better than she does.

One day, Eliza attends a party where there are a lot of delicious homemade snacks. She has an interest in cooking and wonders, how do they know how much to make? The platters never seem to run out and party guests are constantly snacking on delicious treats. One of her favorite snacks at the party is a dip made with artichoke hearts and served with small rounds of thin toast.

Eliza's birthday is coming up, and she decides to serve that artichoke dip to her friends. She wonders how she could make it and how much she would need to prepare. She seeks out the caterer, who gives her a very general recipe, consisting of the ingredients and a description of how the dip should look before and after she bakes it at 350°F in the oven. The caterer makes it on a grand scale for this party, and Eliza wants to do the same for her party. She

Artichoke dip is a great snack for a party. But cooking for a party requires making a much larger amount than a person would usually make for one serving.

really wants this warm, hearty artichoke dip to be a highlight of her party food.

Eliza thinks about how she could use her math skills to estimate how much each guest might eat and how much she should make for the number of guests she plans to invite to her party. She has noticed that she uses math when deciding how long to microwave a snack and for choosing the setting she uses on the stove top for different things, like boiling water or melting butter or chocolate. She even uses math when deciding how long to set the timer for baking goodies in the oven. As Eliza begins to relate to some of these scenarios, she finds that the logic and number sense behind her math problems is starting to fall into place. Eliza will use her passion for cooking to recognize the value of learning the math skills contained within, such as basic operations, working with fractions, estimating, and problem solving.

CHAPTER 1

Kitchen Basics

Before going further into the mathematics of recipe altering and experimentation, Eliza needs to become familiar with some of the kitchen tools she will need for preparing a recipe. A kitchen is stocked with many different implements that serve very specific purposes in cooking and baking.

TOOLS OF THE TRADE

First, bowls of various sizes accommodate different quantities of food. Usually a recipe will call for a particular sized bowl: small, medium, or large, or a very large bowl for recipes that feed a large crowd. A variety of mixing spoons and possibly a whisk should be available. Tongs, spatulas, a strainer, scissors, a sharp knife, and a cutting board are all necessary tools commonly found in the kitchen. Be sure to have an adult su-

A well-stocked kitchen will include a wide variety of tools for cooking. In addition to measuring cups and spoons, knives, cutting boards, graters, and whisks will be on hand.

pervise when a recipe requires chopping. Eliza will need a variety of measuring cups and spoons to accurately measure the ingredients for a recipe.

Measuring cups come in two types: wet and dry measures. Both measures contain eight ounces (oz.) per cup. The wet measures are usually made of glass and have a small spout on one side. They come in one cup, two cup, four cup, and even larger for restaurant kitchens. They are used to measure wet ingredients such as milk, cream, broth, water, or oil. The dry measuring cups measure flour, sugar, and other dry ingredients, and usually come in sizes from 1/4, 1/3, 1/2, to one cup (cup is abbreviated as c; further abbreviations will only list shorthand). There are four 1/4 c in 1 c, three 1/3 c in 1 c, and two 1/2 c in 1 c. Notice the denominator, or the bottom part of the fraction, matches the part of one cup it holds. Use the exact size cup needed and swipe off any overflow with a straight knife run across the top of the cup.

Measuring spoons are essential for getting the right flavor or leavening balance in any recipe. They usually come as a set measuring from ¼, ½, and 1 teaspoon (tsp) and 1 tablespoon (tbsp). Becoming familiar with these measuring devices and their relationships to each other can be a big help in adjusting recipe sizes.

When measuring liquid, there are 2 c in 1 pint (pt) and 2 pt in one quart (qt). These measures come in handy when attempting to

TRY IT YOURSELF: COMPARING MEASURES

Take a measuring tablespoon and a measuring teaspoon (not to be confused with regular eating utensils) and, using water running slowly from a sink faucet, carefully fill the teaspoon and pour the water into the tablespoon. Count the teaspoons until the tablespoon is full. Now take a ¼ c dry or a wet measure and carefully pour one tablespoon at a time into it, counting each one.

1a. How many teaspoons of water will fit into one tablespoon?

1b. How many tablespoons can go into ¼ c?

1c. How many tablespoons are in 1 c?

You can also experiment to discover other relationships. See how many teaspoons fit into a cup before the water spills over and whatever else you can think of.

scale a six-serving recipe up to serve 24 people, for example. If the six-serving recipe calls for 1 c of milk, figure out the scale by dividing 24 by the current serving size: $24 \div 6 = 4$. This means that to increase the quantity to 24 servings, either complete the recipe four times, or save time by multiplying the quantity of each ingredient by 4. For figuring out how much milk to use, the equation $1\ \text{c} \cdot 4 = 4\ \text{c}$ demonstrates the need to use 4 c. And, since there are 4 c for each quart, this recipe scaled up from 6 servings to 24 would need 1 qt of milk.

Suppose a recipe calls for $\frac{2}{3}$ c of butter. It says on the package that one stick of butter is $\frac{1}{2}$ c. The wrap on the butter is usually marked off in tablespoons, specifically eight for a $\frac{1}{2}$ c stick of butter. Two sticks of butter (1 c) contain 16 tbsp so 16 must be divided by 3 in order to know how many tablespoons are in $\frac{1}{3}$ cup: $16 \div 3 = 5\frac{1}{3}$ tbsp. When you double that you get $10\frac{2}{3}$ tbsp. The

Carefully measuring all ingredients is an important step to following a recipe. Another important step is to ask an adult for help, like the girl in this photo *(right)* has done.

wrapper won't give the gradations for $\frac{1}{3}$ tbsp; the only option is to estimate by cutting one of those tablespoons into three equally sized pieces and using two of them.

There is another way to measure ingredients such as butter or shortening or even peanut butter. Take a wet measure cup that holds at least 1 cup more than the amount of the ingredient. Fill it to the 1 cup mark with water, then spoon the shortening or peanut butter into the water until the level reaches 1 $\frac{2}{3}$ c (or 1 c plus the amount of the ingredient being used). At this point, drain the water thoroughly and there will be $\frac{2}{3}$ c of the desired ingredient in the measuring cup. Just be sure to do this with ingredients that are easy to separate from water.

COOKING VERSUS BAKING

Depending on the cook, there are other utensils that will always be useful to have around. A saucepan or even several of different sizes, along with a skillet or two of different sizes, are essential for any cooking on the stove. For people who cater or cook for many people, there are also industrial sized pans, like a 25 qt soup pot. They come in stainless steel, aluminum, non-stick, and endless variations, even cast iron.

It is also important to choose the right sized pan for the recipe. Most recipes will give directions on the size of pan needed and what temperature to set the burner at. Estimating pan size is acceptable. Look at the ingredients that will be going into the pan and compare their volume to the sizes of pans available.

Other kitchen essentials include cake pans and baking pans, and they also come in various shapes and sizes. Circular cake pans

There are many different sizes and styles of pots, saucepans, and skillets to choose from. Some are best for cooking for one, and some are best when cooking for a crowd. Skillets are best for frying, but saucepans are great for various sauces.

are measured by their diameter, their measurement across the middle of the pan. Cookie sheets are long, flat pans with short or no edges. Cookie sheets have many uses besides baking cookies (like pizza or puff pastry treats).

It is important to pre-heat your oven before baking because some ovens will reach high temperatures during the pre-heat to raise the temperature faster and this would affect your baking time. And when baking items such as cookies or cakes, it is very important to follow the directions and measure the ingredients precisely. If too much flour is used, cakes can become heavy and cookies can become hard. So measure all ingredients accurately, and always mix them according to the recipe to ensure that the end result is tasty and the right consistency. The same is true when cooking savory dishes on the stove, such as soup, pasta, or stew.

In all cases, if a recipe is doubled, be sure to write out all the ingredients and multiply them by two so that all amounts are

Some useful baking pans are cookie sheets, bread pans, round and rectangular cake pans, and muffin tins. These come in a variety of materials and sizes.

consistent. If the recipe calls for 1 tsp of baking powder, doubling it will require 2 tsp. This can get tricky when talking about fractions of measurements.

In summary, take an inventory of cooking tools available in the kitchen, experiment with the relationships of various measurements, choose a recipe, and measure carefully. It is recommended that you follow any recipe exactly the first time you make it. Experimentation can take place after the original recipe has yielded success.

CHAPTER 2

RECIPES AND SERVING SIZES

As Eliza ate food in restaurants, in the cafeteria, and at friends' homes, she got more ideas about the foods she wanted to prepare for her party.

She found recipes everywhere. Cookbooks are available from the local library in the 641.5 section of the Dewey Decimal System. Recipes can be found online, on television, and even in magazines and newspapers. There are so many exciting things to cook or bake, from stews, soups, egg dishes, sandwiches, and appetizers to cookies, cakes, custard, and other yummy desserts. There are cookbooks just for desserts or ethnic foods and cookbooks that teach one how to cook and how to experiment and improvise.

Also, all different sorts of cooks write cookbooks, including well known gourmet chefs, TV cooking show stars, creative housewives, and even young adults.

An excellent source for a wide variety of cookbooks is the local library. Many libraries have a section dedicated just to cookbooks.

CHOOSING A RECIPE

To start, choose a recipe with just a few ingredients and uncomplicated preparation. These would be recipes with six or fewer ingredients and short, simple preparations: chop, mix, stir, bake, or cook in saucepan. An example of a more complicated recipe would be one that requires whipping egg whites to a peak and folding them into a batter or cooking different parts separately before combining them. These methods take some experience and practice, so an inexperienced cook shouldn't start here.

Cookbooks specifically written for young people often have tips from more experienced cooks and more explicit directions. They may have a more accurate description of how much time a given recipe will take to prepare for an inexperienced cook. For example, someone new to cooking will not be able to chop as fast as an experienced cook. Most cookbooks tell how many servings the recipe will yield. This gives a baseline from which to scale the recipe to feed the desired number of diners.

The first recipe Eliza chose was the one she found for artichoke dip that sounded just like the one she had at the party. It consisted of six ingredients that should be chopped, minced, grated, and mixed together, and then baked at 350°F for 20–30 minutes. As an inexperienced cook should, Eliza allowed extra time for chopping, mincing, and grating. It could take as long as 30–40 minutes to chop and assemble all ingredients. That's a total of 50 to 70 minutes for this specific recipe.

ADJUSTING THE NUMBER OF SERVINGS

After turning out a delicious dish, it is safe to say that multiplying or dividing all of the ingredients, a process called scaling, will yield the same good food the next time. Write each ingredient and its amount down and then carefully multiply or divide each one by the same number to scale it to the number of servings desired. Doing this ensures that the proportion of ingredients is left unchanged from the original recipe. For example, if the recipe calls for 2 c of flour and 1 ½ tsp of baking powder, then doubling it would require $2 \cdot 2 = 4$ c of flour and $2 \cdot 1\frac{1}{2} = 3$ tsp of baking powder. More experience will make it easier to gauge how much to adjust a recipe. If there is a lot of food left over, perhaps decrease the recipe next time unless it would make a good lunch for the next day.

TRY IT YOURSELF: DOUBLE ELIZA'S RECIPE

Since Eliza decided to double her recipe, she wants to write out the quantity of each ingredient before she starts cooking. The ingredients and their quantities are as follows:

1 15-ounce can of artichoke hearts packed in water, drained and finely chopped
1 tbsp of minced garlic
½ c finely grated Parmesan cheese
½ c mayonnaise
salt and pepper to taste

A closer look at the ingredients showed that some of those that were packaged had extra ingredients, like salt and oil. The recipe didn't say anything about what to do with most

Eliza also had the task of reasoning to determine how much dip she would need to make for her party. The recipe said it should make eight servings. Eliza wanted to have more than enough, so she decided to increase the recipe by half. In an earlier experiment, she followed the recipe exactly as it was and baked it in an 8-inch pie plate. Her family of four consumed six servings. She ultimately decided to double the recipe so that she'd probably have more than she needed.

of those, so Eliza decided to include the ones that were too difficult to separate.

2a. How much of each ingredient would she need to double the recipe?

2b. If she wants the mixture to spread to ¾ inch thick, how big of a pan would she need to use? Keep in mind that this recipe is doubled, so the 8-inch pie plate she used before isn't big enough.

2c. What if she decided to increase the recipe by half? How much of each ingredient would she need?

2d. What size pan should she use for the new scale of 1 ½?

Making a larger amount may require more baking time. But that can be added in small increments (5 – 10 minutes) and by observing the color and texture of the dish as it bakes. Be sure to use a timer.

Another challenge came along when Eliza's friend Wiley won a chili contest: he wanted to make the chili for her. In order to enter the contest, Wiley needed to make 25 quarts of chili. He had to borrow a big pot from Eliza's aunt to fit all of the ingredients for this large amount. It became clear to him that pan size and stove or oven space can be a limiting factor when scaling a recipe to be larger.

Here are the ingredients Wiley used to make 25 qt of chili for the contest:

When scaling a recipe up or down it is important to carefully multiply or divide every ingredient by the same number to ensure the proportions stay the same.

8 pounds (lbs.) ground beef
5 c onion, chopped
5 chopped mild chili peppers
5 – 28–30 ounce (oz.) cans whole tomatoes
5 – 28–30 oz. cans tomato puree
5 – 15 oz. cans each: black beans, pinto beans, and kidney beans.
½ c plus 2 tbsp chili powder
¼ c plus 1 tbsp ground cumin

If Wiley was going to make this chili again, but for Eliza's party, he would need to scale it down to about 5 quarts. So if Wiley typically needs 8 lbs. of ground beef for 25 qts, he needs to divide the total amount of quarts for his original recipe by the amount of quarts he wants to make: 25 qts ÷ 5 qts = 5. Every ingredient must be reduced to a fifth of its size. For the beef: 8÷5 = 1 3/5 lbs. To convert the remaining fraction to ounces, we take the conversion rate of 16 ounces per 1 lb. and apply it to 3/5 of 1 lb.: 16 • 3/5 =

16 • .6 = 1 lb. 9 3/5 oz. Wiley decided to round it off to 1 lb. 8 oz., the equivalent of 1 ½ lbs.

As for the beans, dividing by five shows that each type of bean needs one can. Wiley accidentally bought one more can of black beans than he needed when he made the original recipe, so he just needs one can of pinto beans and one can of kidney beans.

To figure out the chili powder, we can convert to tablespoons and divide. There are 4 tbsp in ¼ c, and the original recipe contained ½ c + 2 tbsp, which converts to 8 tbsp + 2 tbsp, for a total of 10 tbsp chili powder. Divided by five, Wiley would need 2 tbsp of chili powder.

Wiley created a delicious pot of chili both times, but he made a much smaller amount the second time.

Wiley and Eliza are proud of the math skills they have used so far and are eager to plan the next stage of their venture. Coming up on their agenda will be to research the financial aspects of how they can prepare these dishes.

For a big project like chili, it's practical to have a large pot. It's fun to have friends to help complete the job.

CHAPTER 3

SHOPPING, BUDGETING, AND TIMING

Since Eliza and Wiley now know the ingredients and their quantities, it is time to determine how much money they have to spend and prepare a budget. Eliza has $12 to spend on ingredients for her artichoke dip. Her mom already has enough mayonnaise so she just needs artichokes, garlic, and Parmesan cheese. Eliza needs to figure out whether she can buy all those ingredients for $12 or less. Eliza and Wiley will also need to estimate how long it will take to prepare their dishes.

ELIZA'S INGREDIENTS

Eliza and Wiley decide to go on an information gathering expedition to some local markets. Eliza brought her cell phone to take pictures of the prices so they could do their figuring at home.

First, Eliza finds three brands of canned artichoke hearts in water. Some of the store labels contain prices per oz., but Eliza needed to figure this one out for herself. Two of the cans were 14.5 oz. each. One brand cost $3.99 (they were quartered), and the other, a store brand, cost $2.19 (not quartered) per can. The third brand was packaged in a 34 oz. can for $7.99. To figure out what would save the most money, she decided to compare price per oz. of the less expensive brand and the larger can. She would have to divide $2.19 by 14.5 oz. and $7.99 by 34 oz. to get the price per oz. of each size: $2.19 ÷ 14.5 oz. = $.151, or 15 cents per oz. Dividing $7.99 by 34 oz. comes to about $.235 or 24 cents per oz. Number of ounces divided by price would tell how many ounces per dollar, with the bigger comparative answer being the better deal. Usually, the larger sizes are less expensive than the smaller, but as seen here, it is not a good idea to assume that is the case. Do the math.

Next is garlic. They could buy 10 bulbs of garlic for $4 on sale, but they need less than one. Just one bulb costs $.50. To determine which is the cheaper cost for each bulb in the 10 for $4 deal, divide $4.00 by 10. Each bulb costs $.40. Still, they would then be spending an extra $3.50 when they only need one bulb of garlic. They could also get a 6 oz. jar of peeled cloves of garlic for $2.50. That would save a lot of work, but it's still too much garlic. Sometimes the facts have to be weighed. It might be worth it to spend the extra money on nine bulbs of garlic if it is used frequently. Otherwise, it might dry out.

Eliza then finds grated Parmesan cheese. Both brands are $3.99 for 8 oz (approximately 2 c). But Eliza wants to grate authentic Parmesan cheese herself because she thinks it has a better flavor.

Supermarkets carry so many choices of any given product. Prices and amounts vary widely. It is important to research the items one will need to get the desired quality and price.

It cost $15.95 per lb., but she can buy a smaller quantity than that and grate it herself. Eight ounces of grated Parmesan yields about 2 c volume, so 1 c grated would be about 4 oz., or ¼ lb. That would cost her about $4.00 if she estimated ¼ of $15.95 by rounding $15.95 to $16.00 and dividing by four.

WILEY'S INGREDIENTS

Sweet onions are $3.49 or $2.50 per lb. depending on the brand. Regular yellow onions are only $1.49 per lb. Organic yellow onions cost $4.99 per lb. Wiley should also think about what kind of onions would be best for the recipe, and whether or not organic ingredients are important. For example, sweet onions will give a different flavor to the chili than the yellow onions.

He has a choice of 73 percent lean ground beef prepackaged in a tube at $6.69 for 3 lbs., or 80 percent lean ground beef packaged in the store in different quantities for $3.49 per lb. The leanness percentage of the meat tells you how much fat has been ground in with the meat. So Wiley has the choice of buying twice the amount of meat he needs for $6.69 or buying closer to 1 ½ lbs. for approximately 1 ½ x $3.49, which would be roughly $5.25. He also notes that organic lean ground beef costs almost $12.00 per lb. Some would consider this the best bet because of the lack of chemicals both in the meat and in the environment, but as a chef, you have to make your own priorities.

The canned whole tomatoes are priced as follows: the store brand is two for $3.00 or $1.65 for each 28.8 oz. can, while the Italian plum tomatoes are $3.59 for one 30 oz. can. Both brands of tomato puree cost $1.99 per 28.8 or 30 oz. can. Wiley also found 102 oz. cans of tomato products for $3.28. Dividing the cost of the

Ground beef is often packaged in the store and sold in varying weights and proportions of meat and fat. It may appear as 93 percent meat and 7 percent fat or 80 percent meat with 20 percent fat, or some other proportion.

can by the number of ounces determines the price for each ounce. The 102 oz. can is only 3 cents per oz, but 102 oz. is much more than Wiley needs. Organic canned tomatoes range from $2.39 to $3.95 for the same sized can of both whole or tomato puree. A similar process showed him his options for the three types of beans.

Now it is time for some budgeting decisions.

They both calculate what is the least amount of money Wiley will have to spend for his chili. Choosing the lowest priced items on Wiley's list and estimating he would spend $1.00 for 1/3 lb. of poblano peppers, buy 1 lb. of yellow onions, and get the store packaged ground beef in the correct amount (instead of getting a tube of 3 lbs.), his total will come to $13.48. If he wants to purchase

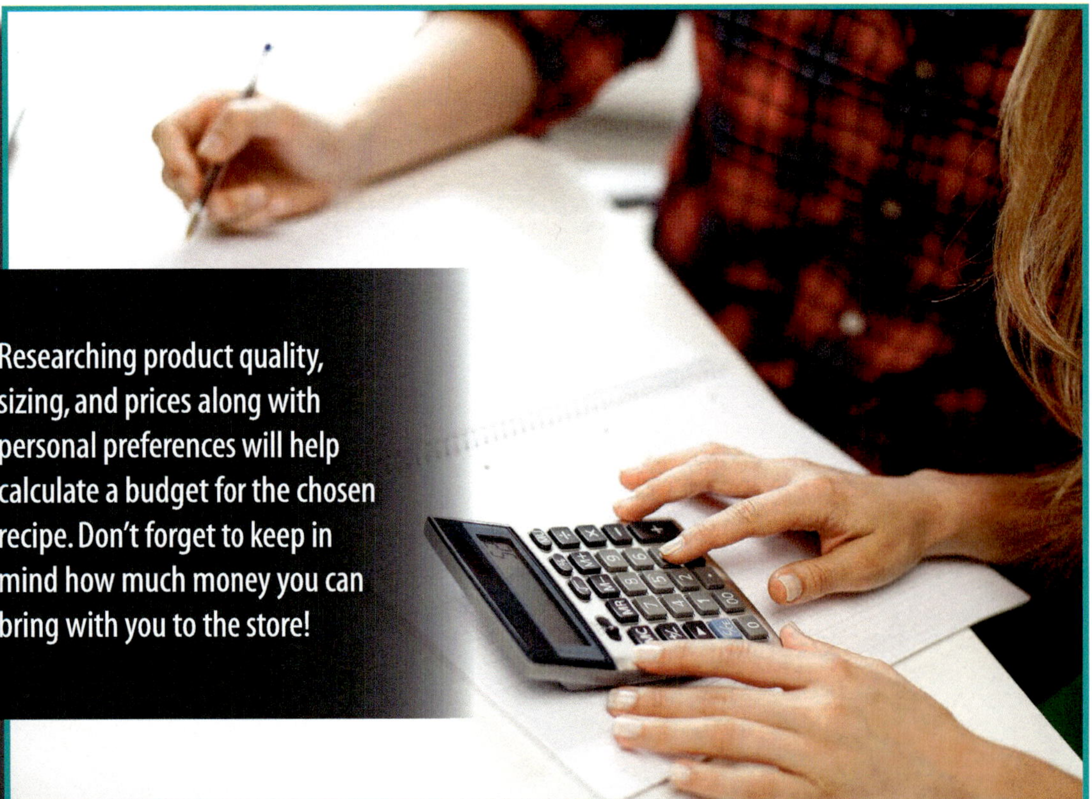

Researching product quality, sizing, and prices along with personal preferences will help calculate a budget for the chosen recipe. Don't forget to keep in mind how much money you can bring with you to the store!

all organic ingredients, he will pay quite a bit more for the ground beef but less than half a dollar more for each can of organic beans. Prices of organic foods are generally higher, but it also depends on the season and the area in which one is shopping.

TRY IT YOURSELF: CAN ELIZA STAY WITHIN HER $12.00 BUDGET?

Eliza needs to buy two small cans of artichoke hearts, 2 tbsp garlic, and ¼ lb. of Parmesan cheese. Note: if 8 oz. of grated Parmesan cheese yields 2 c, then she would only need to buy 4 oz. of ungrated Parmesan cheese to get 1 cup grated.

3a. What is the most she can spend on two small cans of artichoke hearts? What is the least? If she buys the large can of artichoke hearts, how much would that cost?

3b. What is the most she can spend on garlic? What is the least?

3c. Which type of Parmesan cheese can she buy?

3d. What is the difference in price per ounce between grated Parmesan and a chunk of Parmesan of the same weight?

3e. What is her lowest cost to make the dip? What is her highest cost?

TIMING IS EVERYTHING

Eliza knows she has to bake her dip for at least 30 minutes after preparing and mixing all the ingredients. The recipe says it will take her 20 minutes to prepare before baking. She has not yet had a lot of experience chopping or mincing so she is going to estimate it will take her an extra 20 minutes to do all the chopping,

When figuring timing for preparation and serving, a slow cooker can be a handy tool for keeping things warm or starting the dish hours ahead of time.

mincing, and mixing. If she is finished sooner, she can always wait a few minutes to place her dish in the pre-heated oven. If she needs 30 minutes to bake and 20 minutes to prepare, that will add up to 50 minutes. When she adds in the extra 20 minutes prep time plus 10 minutes for the dish to be cool enough to eat, her total time will be 1 hour and 20 minutes. If Eliza wants to present her warm dip at 7:30 p.m., she should begin at 6:10 p.m. to give herself enough time.

As for Wiley, he has decided to make his chili the day before so that he can take his time. He also decided on putting it in a crock pot on low for two hours before the party. His mom said it would be hot enough by then. Both Wiley and Eliza are looking forward to a great party with tasty food.

CHAPTER 4

CONVERSIONS AND OTHER USES FOR MATH IN COOKING

Eliza and Wiley have experimented with the relationships between the different measures used in cooking. They have researched recipes both online and in cookbooks from the library. They both chose recipes they wanted to make. Wiley and Eliza even researched and used their math skills to determine how much they needed to buy, what their respective recipes would cost to make, and the timing needed to have them ready for Eliza's party, which, by the way, was a great success. But the more they cook, the more they encounter new topics to learn about.

METRIC CONVERSIONS FOR COOKING

Wiley encountered a new challenge while visiting friends in Canada. He decided to make his chili recipe for them, but the measurements were all different. For instance, canned goods are measured in grams (g), meat is measured in grams or kilograms (kg), and dry ingredients are measured by weight rather than volume. An example of the difference between weight and volume is opening a new box of cereal or bag of chips and seeing that it is not full. Examining the label will reveal that the product is sold by weight rather than volume.

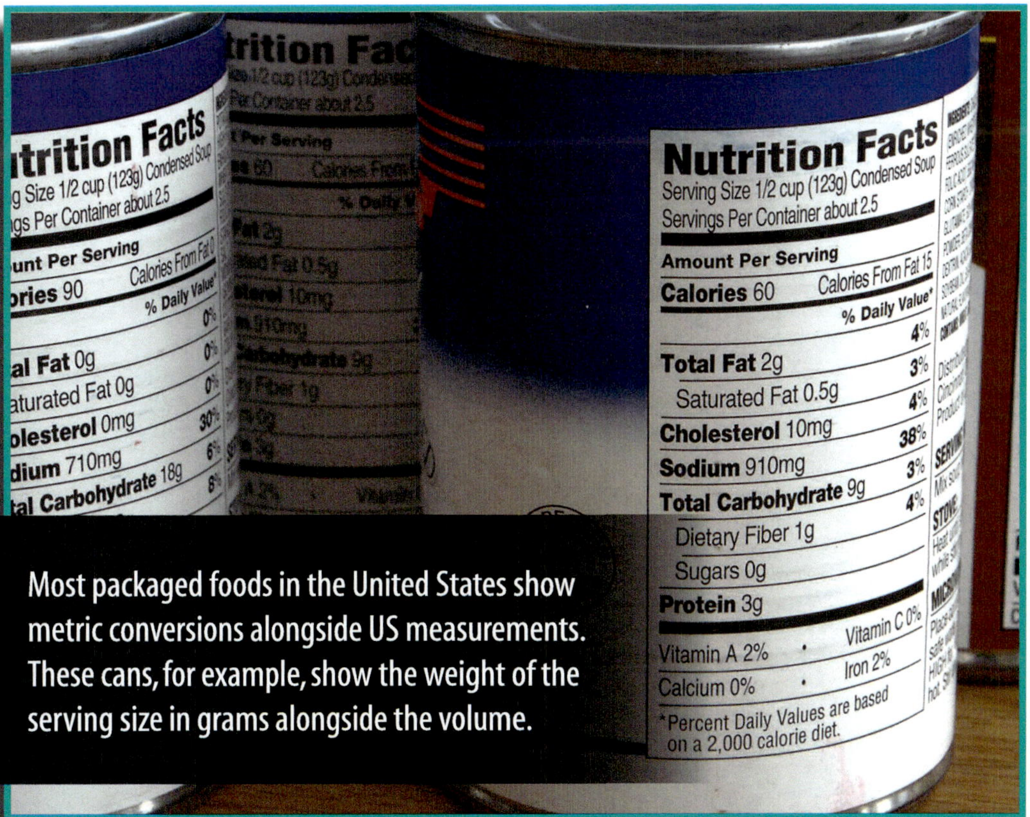

Most packaged foods in the United States show metric conversions alongside US measurements. These cans, for example, show the weight of the serving size in grams alongside the volume.

Wiley's chili recipe calls for 1 ½ lbs. of ground beef. He needs to convert pounds into grams. Since 1 lb. equals 454 g, Wiley needs to buy 1 ½ • 454 g = 681 g of beef for his chili.

He also found canned items measured in grams. The size of cans of tomatoes and tomato puree he usually uses (28.8 to 30 oz.) are 794 g each, and the beans come in 425 g cans (15 oz.). These measurements are included in parentheses on products in the United States by law.

With the help of his friends, who calculated these conversions with him, Wiley was able to create another batch of his chili.

BAKING IN METRICS

Measuring cups measure the volume of an ingredient, while many cooks believe the weight measure is much more accurate. In fact, in the metric system, weight measure is the standard. The example of one ingredient in particular explains the difference of the results of weight versus volume measurement:

When measuring flour with a cup and then weighing it, the weight will vary depending on how the flour is put into the cup. Is it gently scooped in from the top, or is the cup just pushed into the flour bag and pulled up full? Is the excess swiped off with a straight knife or is the cup just shaken to level out the top? Is the flour in the bag fluffed up a little with a spoon before scooping it into the cup or is it packed down in the bag? Weighing cups of flour may produce a difference that is as much as 30 g, depending on how the cup is filled or how densely packed the flour is inside the bag. Thirty grams too much or too little is a massive difference for a measurement that should be exactly 130 g.

Varying density causes the difference in mass in the example of flour. Density is a measurement of how much of a substance's mass is concentrated into a unit of volume, as demonstrated in the equation density = mass ÷ volume. One cup of all-purpose flour is 130 grams while 1 cup of brown sugar is 210 grams. Every item that goes into a cooking or baking project has such a standard of mass that should fill a specific volume, so researching this standard can make recipes even more successful.

Liquid measures are still measured by volume. They come in milliliters (ml) instead of cups or ounces. There are 30 ml in 1 fluid ounce (fl oz.). Although the phrase "fluid ounce" seems to

Wood will float in water because water is denser. But wood will sink in oil because the oil is less dense than wood. Compressing wood's molecules can increase its density, just as packing down the flour made it denser.

imply weight because "ounce" is a measurement of weight, it actually describes volume. Most liquid measuring cups have one side printed with cup measures and ounces while the other side shows milliliters.

Another consideration when baking in a country that uses the metric system is pan size. The 8" x 8" pan Wiley's cornbread recipe calls for would measure 20 cm x 20 cm in the metric system. That is because there are 2.54 cm per inch: 2.54 cm • 8 in = 20.32 cm, and that figure is rounded to an even 20 cm. Use the 2.54 cm per inch conversion factor to convert any size pan to centimeters.

TRY IT YOURSELF: CONVERSIONS

Here is Wiley's list of cornbread ingredients, from a recipe he found online:

1 ½ c milk
2 eggs
⅓ c and 3 tbsp melted butter
1 ½ c flour
⅔ c sugar
½ c cornmeal
1 tbsp baking powder
½ tsp salt

Cornbread is also baked in the oven rather than cooked on the stove. In Canada and many other countries, temperature is labeled as Celsius (°C) instead of Fahrenheit (°F). Wiley is supposed to bake his cornbread in an 8" x 8" square pan at 350°F

SOME OTHER USES FOR MATH IN COOKING

There may, from time to time, be other reasons to use math skills in cooking. For example, sometimes there isn't a full set of measures available. When Eliza was staying at a friend's house and they decided to make a batch of brownies, her friend warned her that she had lost some of the measuring cups. The recipe called for 1 ¼ c of flour, but her friend only had a ⅓ cup measure and one

for about 30 minutes, so he must use the formula (temperature°F-32)(5/9) to convert Fahrenheit to Celsius.

4a. What should Wiley use to measure the milk, and what is the volume of milk that he will need for this recipe?

4b. How many milliliters of melted butter will Wiley need?

4c. If the volume of flour for the cornbread is 1 ½ c, what is the proper weight?

4d. To what temperature will the oven have to be heated in degrees Celsius for the cornbread?

Since he had only just found the recipe for the occasion of his visit to Canada, he couldn't experiment much. He hoped that his friends would eat it and like it.

tablespoon. Eliza realized that there are 4 tablespoons in ¼ cup, so they filled the tablespoon four times with flour. She also realized that filling three 1/3 cup measures would be easier than 16 tablespoons for the additional cup that was required.

Another possible dilemma occurred to Eliza when she was planning to visit friends in Colorado. The place where she would be staying is at an altitude, or height above sea level, that is a little over 7000 feet (ft). Her hometown, on the other hand, is at an altitude that is less than 400 ft. She decided to research baking at high altitude because she knew that the lower air pressure might make a difference in her procedures when she baked for her friends.

When cooking in higher altitudes, the lower air pressure must be considered in a variety of ways; for instance, water will boil at a 198°F at 7,500 feet.

What she found was that baked goods may take longer to bake or temperatures may have to be increased by 25°F for the particular altitude of 7000 ft. Liquids evaporate faster, so she should increase measures of liquids by 3 to 4 tablespoons per cup, and sugar may have to be reduced by 1 to 3 tablespoons per cup. Also, because gases expand more, she must reduce leavening ingredients like baking powder by ¼ teaspoon per teaspoon.

Eliza is now well on her way to appreciating that math really is useful in the real world, and she will continue to study and improve her skills. She has also inspired many of her friends to look at the math involved in their favorite subjects and hobbies.

Answers

Answer 1a. There are 3 teaspoons in 1 tablespoon. So if a recipe calls for 1 tsp of some ingredient, to serve three times as many servings, triple the portion of that ingredient by using 1 tbsp.
Answer 1b. Four tablespoons filled the ¼ cup or filled to the ¼ cup line in the wet measure.
Answer 1c. Count how many tablespoons fit, or solve for tablespoons per cup. If four ¼ c make 1 c, then 4 • 4 tbsp make 1 c. Multiply 4 (¼ c per cup) x 4 (tbsp per ¼ c) to isolate tablespoons per cup. There are 16 tbsp in one cup.

Answer 2a. 2 – 15-ounce cans of artichoke hearts, drained and finely chopped
2 tbsp of minced garlic
1 c of finely grated Parmesan cheese
1 c of mayonnaise
salt and pepper to taste
Answer 2b. Doubling the area of the circular pan's base would allow the mixture to spread to ¾ inch thick. The area of the circular pan's base is $\pi r^2 = \pi 4^2 = 16\pi = 50.265$ in^2, so doubling that to 100.53in^2 is the area of a baking pan she should use. Next, she'll need to know the dimensions of that pan. A square pan would need the dimensions $\sqrt{(100.53\text{in}^2)}$ = 10.02in x 10.02in, but a 9" x 13" baking pan (117in^2) would be close enough. A circular pan's radius can be found by working backward: if πr^2 = 100.53in^2, divide by π and find the square root for a radius measurement of 5.66in (estimate up or down to find pan size and increase time for 5in pan or decrease for 6in pan).

Answer 2c. To increase it by ½, she would have to multiply everything by 1 ½, so she would need:
1 ½ cans of artichoke hearts
1 ½ tbsp of minced garlic
¾ c of grated Parmesan cheese
¾ c of mayonnaise
salt and pepper to taste
Answer 2d. A pie plate of approximately 10 in.

Answer 3a. 2 x 3.99 = $7.98 is the highest price; $4.38 is the lowest price for two small cans. Buying the bulk can would cost her $7.99, almost the same as two of the highest priced small cans. But with 2 x 14.5 = 29 oz. and the bulk containing 34 oz. she would have 34 – 29 = 5 extra ounces of artichoke hearts.
Answer 3b. Eliza can get a lot of garlic for $4.00. But she only needs 2 tbsp, which she can easily get from 1 bulb with some to spare for $.50. The best deal per bulb would be 10 bulbs for $4.00, which equals 40 cents per bulb, but she can reduce her overall cost by $3.50 by going with the single bulb for $.50.
Answer 3c. Eliza can purchase Parmesan cheese that is already grated or she can buy a solid chunk that she would have to grate herself.
Answer 3d. The already grated Parmesan comes in a container holding 8 oz., and costs at least $3.99, or $3.99 per pack. The equation $3.99 ÷ 8 shows that each ounce is about $.50. A pound of Parmesan is $15.95 per lb., or $15.95 per 16 oz. So, $15.95 ÷ 16 shows that each ounce is close to $1.00.

Answer 3e. To find her lowest cost to make the dip, she adds up the lower priced ingredients: $4.38 (artichoke hearts) + $0.50 (garlic) + $3.99 (Parmesan cheese) = $8.87. She will even have some money left over.

Her highest cost would be $7.98 (artichoke hearts) + $4.00 (garlic) + $4.00 (Parmesan cheese) = $15.98, and this is over her budget.

Answer 4a. Milk is a liquid measure, so use the glass measuring cup. On the metric side, it is clear that 1 ½ c is equal to 360 ml. Or, calculate this conversion as follows: 30 ml per oz for 12 oz. figures into the equation 30 ml per oz. • 12 oz = 360 ml.

Answer 4b. Convert ⅓ c to ml by taking the conversion rate of 8 oz. per cup and 30 ml per ounce: 8 oz. x 30 ml per oz. = 240 ml per cup; now, milliliters per cup multiplied by the number of cups will describe the grand total milliliters for the ⅓ cup portion of the amount of butter: 240 ml per cup • ⅓ cup = 80 ml. For the 3 tbsp, we can make that a fraction of a cup. Sixteen tablespoons = 1 cup, so 3 tbsp = 3⁄16 c. Like ⅓ c, we can multiply the number of cups against 240 ml per cup to convert the 3 tbsp to ml: 3⁄16 c • 240 ml per cup = 45 ml. The grand total of ⅓ cup and 3 tbsp is equal to their converted figures in ml: 80 ml + 45 ml = 125 ml.

Answer 4c. Using the conversion of 1 c of flour per 120 g, multiply 120 g by 1 ½ for your answer: 180 g.

Answer 4d. Using the formula (temperature°F-32)(5 ÷ 9), substitute 350 for the temperature and solve for degrees Celsius: (350-32)(5 ÷ 9) = 177°C.

GLOSSARY

ALTITUDE The height above sea level.

BUDGET The amount of money that is available for a particular purpose.

CHOPPED Cut into small pieces with a knife, as when preparing ingredients for cooking.

CONSISTENCY The thickness or density of a mix of ingredients.

DENOMINATOR The bottom number of a fraction denoting the number of pieces the whole is cut into.

DENSITY A measurement of how much mass occupies a specific volume: mass/volume.

ESSENTIAL Necessary or needed.

ESTIMATE To use an inexact figure in place of an exact figure, usually for when you don't have the means or time to calculate exactly (for example, describing being hungry enough to eat about two plates of food, or guessing how many pieces of rice are in a pot).

GRAM A metric measure of weight that is equal to 1/1000 of a kilogram (a kilogram converts to 2.2 pounds, so a gram is also 1/1000 of 2.2 lbs.).

GRATED Cut into very small pieces by rubbing against a rough surface, as when preparing ingredients for cooking.

IMPLEMENT A useful tool or utensil.

LEAVENING An agent such as baking powder that produces gas to lighten dough or batter.

MASS The measurement of particles than an object has; what remains of an object's weight without the force of gravity.

MILLILITER A liquid metric measure equal to one thousandth of a liter.

MINCED Very finely chopped or cut into tiny pieces.

ORGANIC Grown without pesticides or artificial fertilizers.

PRE-HEAT To allow an oven or other device to heat up to a temperature before using that device.

PROPORTION The uniform amount of different items that contribute to a whole, like two hydrogen molecules and an oxygen molecule making a single water molecule.

SAVORY An appealing taste or smell; a pleasant flavor that is not sweet.

SIMMER To heat something just below boiling.

SPATULA A wide, flat kitchen tool used to flip items in a pan or to scrape something from a surface.

STRAINER A bowl-like device with holes all over the surface for draining liquids from cooked food.

TONGS A hinged hand device for picking up food or objects that would otherwise be messy (like chicken) or dangerous (like poison) to handle.

VOLUME The amount of space that an object takes up.

WHISK A stirring device made of several looped wires on a handle that is used to whip or beat ingredients.

For More Information

Canadian Mathematical Society
209-1725 St. Laurent Boulevard
Ottawa, ON K1G 3V4
Canada
(613) 733-2662
Website: http://cms.math.ca
This society supports math education by working with and supporting math educators. One of its purposes is to raise understanding and enthusiasm for math in students.

ChopChopKids
695-697 Belmont Street
Belmont, MA 02478
(617) 924-3993
Website: http://www.chopchopmag.org
This nonprofit organization is dedicated to teaching kids and families to cook real food together. They seek to make a difference in the obesity and hunger epidemics that plague parts of our world.

The MathCounts Foundation
1420 King Street
Alexandria, VA 22314
(703) 299-9006
Website: https://www.mathcounts.org
This foundation's goal is to increase interest and confidence in math and problem solving for middle schoolers. It sponsors in-person math contests.

National Council for Teachers of Mathematics
1906 Association Drive
Reston, VA 20191
(800) 235-7566
Website: http://www.nctm.org
This council is dedicated to providing teachers with support to ensure quality mathematics education to all students.

The Young Peoples' Project (TYPP)
The Westside Commons
696 Amsterdam Avenue
New York, NY
(212) 874-7272
Website: http://www.typp.org
This organization trains math literacy workers, and helps students in Chicago, Boston, Mississippi, New York, and San Francisco succeed regardless of ethnicity, gender, or class.

WEBSITES

Because of the changing nature of internet links, Rosen Publishing has developed an online list of websites related to the subject of this book. This site is updated regularly. Please use this link to access the list:

http://www.rosenlinks.com/MYWAU/cooking

For Further Reading

Bayden, Maya, and James Toriello. *The Stomach in 3D*. New York, NY: Rosen Publishing, 2016.

Einhorn, Edward. *Fractions in Disguise: A Math Adventure*. Watertown, MA: Charlesbridge Publishing, 2014.

Ellis, Julie. *Pythagoras and the Ratios: A Math Adventure*. Watertown, MA: Charlesbridge Publishing, 2014.

Ganeshram, Ramin, and Jean Paul Vellotti (photographer). *FutureChefs: Recipes by Tomorrow's Cooks Across the Nation and the World*. Emmaus, PA: Rodale Books, 2014.

Gardner, Jane P. *Food Science* (Science 24/7). Broomall, PA: Mason Crest Publishers, 2015.

Levy, Joel. *Exploring the Mysteries of Mathematics*. New York, NY: Rosen Publishing, 2017.

McKellor, Danica. *Girls Get Curves*. New York, NY: Penguin Group, 2012.

Neuschwander, Cindy. *Sir Cumference and the Viking's Map*. Watertown, MA: Charlesbridge Publishing, 2012.

Sitwell, William. *A History of Food in 100 Recipes*. New York, NY: Little, Brown and Company, 2013.

Wilson, Bee. *Consider the Fork: A History of How We Cook and Eat*. New York, NY: Basic Books, 2013.

Bibliography

Burns, Marilyn. *About Teaching Mathematics: A K-8 Resource*. 2nd ed. Sausalito, CA: Math Solutions Publications, 2000.

Burns, Marilyn. *The I Hate Mathematics! Book*. New York, NY: Little, Brown and Company, 1975.

Burns, Marilyn. *Math for Smarty Pants*. New York, NY: Little, Brown and Company, 1982.

Burns, Marilyn. *Writing in Math Class: A Resource for Grades 2–8*. Sausalito, CA: Math Solutions Publications, 2002.

Carle, Megan, Jill Carle, with Judi Carle. *Teens Cook: How to Cook What You Want to Eat*. Berkeley, CA: Ten Speed Press, 2004.

Epidemiology & Community Health Research at the University of Minnesota. "Project EAT." University of Minnesota. Retrieved December 7, 2016. http://www.sphresearch.umn.edu/epi/project-eat.

Iowa State University Extension and Outreach. "Food and Nutrition." Iowa 4-H. Retrieved December 7, 2016. http://www.extension.iastate.edu/4h/projects/foodandnutrition.

Lee, Sandra. *Semi-Homemade Cool Kids' Cooking*. Des Moines, IA: Meredith Books, 2006.

Mayhew, Maggie (consultant), and Francesca Baines (senior editor). *How to Cook*. New York, NY: DK Publishing, 2011.

Munsen, Sylvia. *Cooking the Norwegian Way*. Minneapolis, MN: Lerner Publications Company, 1982.

Musser, Gary L., William F. Burger, and Blake E. Peterson. *Mathematics for Elementary Teachers: A Contemporary Approach*. New York, NY: John Wiley & Sons, 2001.

Rivera, Ada. "Measuring Measurement." University of Houston. Retrieved December 7, 2016. http://atlantis.coe.uh.edu/archive/science/science_lessons/scienceles3/measure.

Sheen, Barbara. *Foods of Cuba*. New York, NY: Kidhaven Press, 2011.

Watson, Stephanie. "Organic Food No More Nutritious Than Conventionally Grown Food." Harvard Health Publications, September 5, 2012. http://www.health.harvard.edu/blog/organic-food-no-more-nutritious-than-conventionally-grown-food-201209055264.

Wonderopolis. "How Can Math Help You Cook?" Retrieved September 3, 2016. http://wonderopolis.org.

Index

ABOUT THE AUTHOR

Linda R. Baker holds a bachelor of science degree in education and math. Math confused her as a child, but she rediscovered it in college when she had a professor who could explain things in ways she could understand. Since then, she has been enthusiastically teaching and tutoring math to students of all ages and abilities. She is a lifelong learner who enjoys reading, writing, and artistic pursuits in her spare time. She now resides in Florida and enjoys teaching math to adults with special needs.

PHOTO CREDITS

Cover, p. 1 Hero Images/Getty Images; p. 5 MSPhotographic/iStock/Thinkstock; p. 7 Ruslan Grumble/Shutterstock.com; p. 9 Tyler Olson/Shutterstock.com; p. 11 Naruedom Yaempongsa/Shutterstock.com; p. 12 Chas53/iStock/Thinkstock; p. 14 Stockbyte/Thinkstock; p. 18 Joshua Resnick/Shutterstock.com; p. 19 Westend61/Getty Images; p. 22 Ciaran Griffin/Stockbyte/Thinkstock; p. 23 hacohob/Shutterstock.com; p. 24 Syda Productions/Shutterstock.com; p. 26 Devrim_Pinar/iStock/Thinkstock; p. 29 Rob Byron/Shutterstock.com; p. 31 Kino/VWPics/Age Fotostock; p. 34 © iStockphoto.com/TomBegasse; interior pages background Marina Sun/Shutterstock.com.

Designer: Brian Garvey; Layout Designer: Greg Tucker; Editor: Bernadette Davis; Photo Researcher: Sherri Jackson